The
ARMCHAIR
CONDUCTOR

HOW TO LEAD A SYMPHONY ORCHESTRA IN THE PRIVACY OF YOUR OWN HOME

The ARMCHAIR CONDUCTOR

How To lead A Symphony Orchestra In The Privacy Of Your Own Home

Dan Carlinsky and Ed Goodgold

Titan Books
LONDON

THE ARMCHAIR CONDUCTOR
ISBN 1 85286 539 3

Published by
Titan Books Ltd
42-44 Dolben Street
London SE1 0UP

First Titan edition June 1994
10 9 8 7 6 5 4 3 2 1

British Library Cataloguing-in-Publication Data. A catalogue record for this book is
available from the British Library.

Printed and bound by Wiltshire (Bristol) Limited, Philip Street, Bedminster, Bristol.

LADIES AND GENTLEMEN: VICTOR BORGE

My experience with Armchair Conducting goes back only about seventy years, at the most. The "orchestra" consisted of my older brother, Sven, who donated his services with the help of a broom, a cane, and cello motions. He sat there attentively as I waved the baton to recorded music we heard on the gramophone. If I found a tempo too slow or too fast, boy, did my brother get yelled at!! Since those days, my orchestras have grown considerably. Sven would have been proud. And relieved!

Armchair Conducting is invigorating, enjoyable, and healthful. I heartily recommend it whether you have an older brother or not.

OVERTURE

You can draw a sort of immense emotional throb out of the air merely by curving your hand. You can get brilliant waves of sound merely by a twist of the wrist. You can make sudden and absolute silence by a gesture. It is the most wonderful of all sensations that any man can conceive. It really oughtn't to be allowed.

—*Sir Eugene Goossens*

Music isn't just for listening.

Whether you're hearing the Boston Symphony or the band at your cousin's wedding, first your foot starts tapping. Then your hands keep time too. And before you know it, you're conducting . . . sort of.

In the privacy of your own home—where no one can see—you like to lead the orchestra. You're an Armchair Conductor.

You might gyrate like Leonard Bernstein in his heyday at the New York Philharmonic or bounce to a Latin rhythm like Ricky Ricardo at the Tropicana.

Wouldn't you like to learn to do it right?

A pleasant evening or two at home with this book and you'll be waving your baton with aplomb, cuing the horns, shushing the timpani, and making all sorts of other very impressive moves. You don't have to be an accomplished musician to look like a pro—in fact, you don't even have to know how to read music. All you need to do is follow this book, your ears and your heart.

By the time you finish reading, you and your baton will be making beautiful music together.

The Thrill of Conducting

- ENJOY the power of leading the world's top musical aggregations—without having to wear formal clothes.
- ENTERTAIN your friends in the comfort of your own living room or recreational vehicle with your mastery of music's mysterious sign language.
- EXERCISE through art!
- ENLARGE your cocktail-party repertoire with an assortment of anecdotes about celebrated conductors.
- ENTER the musical Twilight Zone, where the rolling wave of music meets the tip of the baton to form a splendid illusion.

Where To Do It

- AT HOME, in your armchair. (Of course.)
- IN YOUR SEAT at the concert hall. (Don't disturb your neighbors—use your index finger.)
- IN YOUR CAR at stoplights or in traffic jams. (Otherwise, keep both hands on the wheel.)
- IN STORES, RESTAURANTS, AND ELEVATORS. (Ignore the boors who stare—they're just envious of your Muzak technique.)
- ON THE PHONE when you're put on hold with recorded music. (Don't curse it—conduct it.)

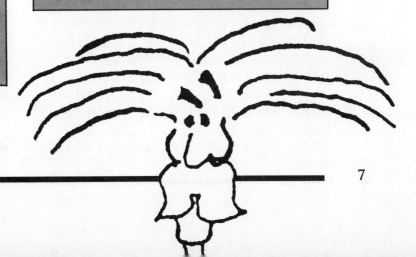

A PAINLESS HISTORY OF CONDUCTING

In the beginning, there were no conductors. Who needed them? Music was a couple of guys sitting around the cave plucking, strumming, and thumping stones, branches, and various portions of animal innards. By the time the Egyptians, Hebrews, and Greeks came along, the slicker musical groups designated someone to keep time by clapping hands or tapping a stick on the ground, but by and large musical performances were like jam sessions. After a while, the size of musical aggregations increased, and so did the complexity of the music. Someone really had to step in and keep order.

In the Middle Ages, choir leaders sometimes beat the pulse of the music with a stick and in some monasteries, monks were led in chant by a brother who used hand signals to indicate not only the beat but the melody. For the next few hundred years, musical performances often were coordinated by a musician clapping his hands, stamping his feet, and pounding a big stick on his music stand to keep the rhythm. This tended to wear out a lot of music stands and sometimes annoyed audiences by drowning out the music. During Bach's time, it was common for the harpsichordist to keep things going smoothly from the keyboard; when Haydn and Mozart were at the top of the Top Forty, the number one

The most bombastic of the nineteenth-century virtuoso composer-conductors, Hector Berlioz

Leading the band, early-fourteenth-century style

violinist usually did the honors, using his bow. Sometimes a keyboardist and a fiddler tried to share the responsibility. That, as you might imagine, could give rise to friction.

As orchestras grew even larger and music began to need interpretation as well as organization, performances began to be led by a nonplaying music man, usually the composer. No one can blame the composer for getting into the act, since he didn't know *what* might happen if he let the musicians out of his sight. In the 1800s, a light, manageable version of the old big stick—the baton—became the rule; it was used to beat the air, not the ground. Until this point, conductors commonly stood off to one side or faced the audience, not the orchestra. But soon they turned around and got serious. Then the Age of Specialization hit, with the development of the full-time interpretative conductor. By the end of the 1800s the conductor had become the real star of the show, a soloist whose instrument was the whole orchestra.

And here we are.

LIVE LONG AND PROSPER:
CONDUCTING YOUR WAY TO BETTER HEALTH

There is a long and impressive list of prominent conductors who beat time to age eighty, eighty-five, or beyond—until time finally beat them. The roster includes Arturo Toscanini, Otto Klemperer, Pierre Monteux, Bruno Walter, Ernest Ansermet, Sir Thomas Beecham, Sir Adrian Boult, Leopold Stokowski, Tullio Serafin, André Kostelanetz, Fred Waring, Pablo Casals, Hans Knappertsbusch, and Arthur Fiedler, who in his late seventies began spouting this motto:

> "He who rests rots."

Leopold Stokowski (b. 1882, d. 1977)

Arthur Fiedler (b. 1894, d. 1979)

Why do so many conductors outwit the actuaries? Perhaps it is the occupation itself. "I have an energetic job," said Sir Malcolm Sargent, who could have been speaking for all his fellow conductors. "I spend up to six hours a day waving my arms about. If everyone else did the same, they would stay much healthier. I don't have to play golf to get exercise." His colleague Sir John Barbirolli said the same thing, but in a more earthy fashion: "You know why conductors live so long? Because we perspire so much."

Before he took over the Boston Pops, John Williams suggested that then-director Arthur Fiedler, performing six concerts a week in season, was expending energy equivalent to pitching five or six baseball games a week, something no ballplayer would ever dream of doing. (Still, Williams was willing to take the job after Fiedler died at eighty-five.)

The physical aspect of conducting isn't always recognized by outsiders. Sir Thomas Beecham used to tell of the time he gave a baton to a professional boxer, telling him, "Wave that about and see how long you can keep it up." The fighter lasted, according to Sir Thomas, nine minutes—about one fifth the length of a Mahler symphony. Leading an orchestra, of course, does often require great stamina, and is rigorously aerobic.

That serious conducting can be a real work-out is attested to by James Levine, for whom perspiration requires a complete change of clothes, from underwear to tie, after every opera act, and by Leonard Slatkin, who maintains that he loses two to three pounds a concert, "depending on the music and the shirt I wear."

If you take up Armchair Conducting with a passion, will you live longer than your genetic and environmental histories might indicate? It couldn't hurt.

Get Ready

To be a competent real-life conductor, you need—besides incredibly broad musical talents, charisma, and a tux—the skill to do more than one thing at a time, both physically and mentally. You need the ability to make totally different gestures with both arms simultaneously. And, at the same time, you have to be able to think about the notes

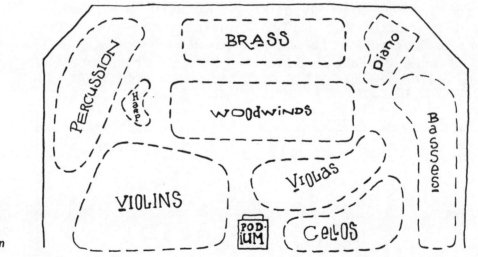

Sample Symphony Orchestra Seating Plan

coming up while you pay scrupulous attention to the notes being played *right now*.

As an Armchair Conductor you may not be so gifted. But you can learn to fake it.

Not that you'll be able to step up in front of the Cleveland Orchestra and make them believe. But with practice, you'll be able to grab your baton and ride through your favorite recordings, *feeling* like a conductor. You'll impress your friends, get your blood flowing, and feel the power.

**Sample
Living Room
Orchestra
Seating Plan**

About Batons

Time beaters in early musical aggregations used a stick or, occasionally, a roll of sheet music or other paper. During the mid-nineteenth century, the baton as we know it became pretty much standard: a thin, usually white stick of wood (these days sometimes of fiberglass), tapered and with a swollen or bulb-shaped handle of wood, cork, plastic, or rubber.

Dedicated conductors often use batons that are precisely measured and matched, custom designed and crafted, even painted to order. Of concern in the process of fine-tuning a baton are variables such as size, shape, and fleshiness of the palm; the kind of music to be conducted; and the user's technique. Conductors debate materials, weights, and handle shapes (ball? egg? pear? teardrop? cattail?). Batons come in many sizes, but as any musician will tell you, it isn't the size that counts—it's what you do with it.

Conducting with an old-style giant baton in the early sixteenth century

16

Composer
Carl Maria
von Weber
directing
with a
paper roll
(1826)

Niccolò
Paganini,
the legendary
Italian
violinist,
using his
bow (1830s)

Giuseppe Verdi
attracting
attention with
an ebony
baton (1879)

HOW TO HOLD THE BATON

The right hand does the conductor's basic work. If you're left handed, that's your tough luck. Yes, it's true that Paul McCartney has made more money than many nations have in their treasuries, proving that left-handed guitarists can succeed if they're cute. And there have been violinists who've turned their strings around and played backward with great success. But to *conduct* left handed is to court disaster: musicians have enough problems without having to watch a conductor in reverse.

(If you're a lefty who can't even drink a glass of water right handed, go ahead and Armchair-Conduct with your left hand—you won't confuse the CD. But you'll have to go through this book with a pencil doing plenty of changing "left" to "right" and vice versa. Lots of luck.)

Here's how to meet and greet your baton:

Put the handle in the lower palm of your

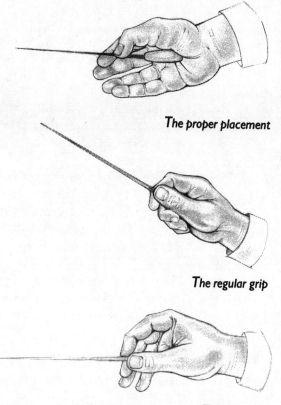

The proper placement

The regular grip

The light grip

right hand, near the heel of the hand, and lay the beginning of the shaft lightly between the ball of your thumb and the side of the first crease of your index finger. Bend the index finger halfway to the palm; wrap the remaining fingers around the handle as far as they go. The tip of the ring finger should touch your palm.

Shake hands with the baton. As you conduct, your palm will face left, down, or in between, depending on what moves it's making, but the basic position is palm down.

(For especially soft, lyrical passages, you can shift your bent index finger to the top of the shaft, put the thumb on the side, and loosen the other fingers, letting the pinkie float freely. But don't spend too much time at first learning this secondary grip—you'll be fine without it.)

Other things to remember about batonmanship:

- Keep the baton pointing slightly left of straight ahead.
- Don't hold the end of the handle with your fingertips.
- Don't let the handle lose contact with your palm.
- Don't squeeze.

A word of advice: Some blue-chip conductors hold their batons in an unorthodox fashion, much as some top tennis players use a two-handed backhand and an occasional pro golfer uses an odd grip with a wood. These are highly talented people who succeed in spite of their offbeat methods, not because of them. *You* are better off sticking to the book. No offense.

SUBSTITUTE STICKS

What does the unfortunate conductor do when the urge strikes but there isn't a baton in sight?

Eve Queler once was asked to conduct a New York City Opera rehearsal on such short notice that she was forced to use a pencil. José Iturbi, the Spanish pianist who became famous playing himself in 1940s movie musicals, once did a bit of rehearsal conducting with a cigar stub in place of a baton. As a child, Catherine Comet used to entertain an audience of one—her mother—with music she conducted with a chopstick. And James Levine remembers sitting in Cincinnati Symphony concerts at age nine, conducting with one of his mother's knitting needles.

The Armchair Conductor's alternatives are many. Pencils and pens are most popular. (For safety and neatness, pencils should be unsharpened and pens should be used only if out of ink, since even the most tightly screwed-on cap may spin off during "The Stars and Stripes Forever.") A screwdriver can be a good substitute for a home handyman looking to lead the band in the workshop; try a Phillips-head.

Certain foods can do in a pinch. In some areas, dried pasta is popular; a sturdy spaghettoni is advisable. (Capellini, vermicelli, and other delicate shapes should be used only to direct slow movements.)

French conductors call the stick a *baguette*, after the long bread of that name; come to think of it, you could use a thin bread in a pinch—preferably day old. Long Italian breadsticks make an even better shape, although they present two possible hazards:

1. Sesame sticks can launch a hail of seeds during a rollicking passage, and

2. The self-control of an Armchair

Conductor beating time with a garlic or onion breadstick is seldom sufficient to get through even a short movement with breadstick intact and in hand, rather than in mouth.

Vegetables make the healthiest substitute batons: a stalk of celery or a carrot, an ear of corn (husked), a slender zucchini (favored by gardeners in late harvest season). There's nothing like conducting your favorite overture right before ingesting your minimum daily requirement of fiber.

GETTING IN SHAPE

To obtain flexibility for proper baton handling, no special equipment is required. You need not even have your baton with you. These exercises may be done anytime, anywhere:

1. Hold your baton or a pencil in the correct grip, then roll it quickly back and forth

between the thumb and the index finger. Try to keep the wrist and arm stationary.

2. Now point the stick straight ahead and move it up and down several times, again without using your wrist and arm.

3. And move the stick side to side, far left to far right, finger action only.

4. And, again with fingers only, move the stick in circles—first smaller, then slowly larger, aiming for the largest circumference you can reach without getting your wrist involved. Clockwise and counterclockwise.

5. Now, repeat exercises 2, 3, and 4, using some wrist action but no forearm. If you must, hold your baton arm at the elbow with your left hand to keep it from joining the action.

6. Repeat the three exercises—up and down, side to side, circle—letting the forearm get into the act.

7. And repeat all three using the whole arm, from the shoulder.

8. A whole-body limber-up to use before a conducting session:
- Stand straight with both arms slightly away from the sides.
- Start shaking your arms, ever more vigorously and loosely, until they fairly flop around.
- Slowly tighten up on the control until you are shaking them only slightly.
- Stop shaking and drop your arms.

9. And another:
- Hold both arms above the head; inhale.
- Exhale and suddenly drop them down to your sides.
- Repeat several times.

Those who are too busy to set aside regular exercise time specifically designed for baton conditioning can fit appropriate exercise into their daily lives. Here are some extra-

musical activities that will help improve
your conducting fitness:

- knitting
- polishing silver
- carving scrimshaw
- whipping cream
- shucking corn
- kneading dough
- scrambling eggs (or, for cholesterol
  watchers, egg whites)
- removing worn-out light bulbs
- replacing them

THE RIGHT HAND

Here's what the conductor's right hand does:
- Holds the baton.
- Starts the music and stops the music.
- Keeps the music going in between by marking the beat.
- Sets the tempo. (Some people think that's all the conductor does—acts as a human metronome or, as one cynic put it, a "pendulum in white tie and tails." Setting the pace *is* an important function, but it's by no means the only one.)
- Determines whether the music is loud or soft.
- Determines whether the music is snappy or schmaltzy.
- Indicates accents and pauses.
- Hands out cues—sometimes.

Right-hand work has to come so easily you can just about switch to automatic pilot and concentrate on the left hand.

THE LEFT HAND

Conducting requires a happy marriage between the right hand and the left, much like a husband and wife who have things worked out in the kitchen: one washes, the other dries. While the right hand gets the music going and keeps it going, the left takes care of the crucial details and side issues. The left hand:
- Gives most of the cues.
- Helps control the volume.
- Helps control the tempo.
- At times, for emphasis, mimics the baton with mirror-image motions, especially in starting and stopping the music and in announcing important changes in rhythm or speed.
- In the case of show orchestras and jazz bands, signals spur-of-the-moment decisions; in the case of school wind-bands and other amateur groups, helps the musicians find their way around the

written music.
- Turns pages of the score.
- Pulls a handkerchief out of a pocket, wipes perspiration off the conductor's forehead, and replaces the handkerchief.
- Scratches.

More later.

THE EYES

"Half our trade is in the eyes," Zubin Mehta once told an interviewer. "There is an implicit trust and understanding between conductor and musician that cannot be imparted with the hands alone. And you cannot have a conversation onstage."

It's human nature to make eye contact with someone standing in front of you. Most successful conductors know how to make this connection pay off, from a simple glance-as-cue (in place of a gesture) to outright intimidation. Silently and instantly, the eyes can say things like "Here comes the passage we rehearsed all afternoon, and if you flub it you'll be looking for work in the morning." Riccardo Muti's imperious glare, for example, has been called "the Death Ray." Other prominent conductors boast similar ocular prowess.

For their part, good musicians, no matter how hard they're focusing on their music, always keep the baton within the field of

Here, Riccardo Muti considerately protects the orchestra from his Death Ray glare by conducting with his eyes closed.

their peripheral vision, constantly glancing at the conductor's face to see what's going on.

As an Armchair Conductor, of course, you have no prima donnas to put in their place, or sniveling last-chair violists to turn into mincemeat. But that doesn't mean you can't use your eyes. A raised eyebrow here, a scowl there—a little well-placed eye action really helps make you look the part. That's acting, you say? Of course it is.

USING YOUR BODY

At music schools, conducting students are strongly advised not to gyrate, not to hop around. Half a century ago, the author of an English conducting text warned against "astonishing and bewildering stick-and-body acrobatics." Even though some audiences are impressed, he counseled, "avoid these like the plague; you are an artist—not a circus performer."

The Armchair Conductor, on the other hand, is forgiven a bit of extra motion. A little "acrobatics" can distract from any mistakes your arms are making and, if done right, can reflect the emotion of the music. Unless you're an unusually fast learner, you won't be able to do nearly as much with your arms as a pro, so why not make up for that lack with a little tasteful gyrating?

(**Note:** The preceding generous allowance is not a license to imitate Leonard Bernstein. On him it always looked good; on *you* it would look as though you're standing on the runway in the fog bringing in a plane that's lost radio contact with the control tower. Nor is this modest suggestion an invitation to flap wildly like a four-year-old at a concert in the park. When a four-year-old mock-conducts, people smile and say, "Isn't that cute?" They won't say that about you. Reread the preceding paragraph: you are being given dispensation, it says, to use *a bit*

of extra body English. Please—don't abuse the privilege.)

ATTITUDE

It sometimes seems that on the list of required attributes for conductors, musical talent must share top billing with having a fine opinion of oneself. To the Armchair Conductor, musical talent isn't a necessity, but a healthy ego certainly is.

If great teachers teach by example, the four great conductors in these anecdotes qualify as great teachers. You can learn all you need to know about ego from them:

Sir Thomas Beecham had just led a performance of a Mozart opera, one of his specialties. Backstage, he was duly congratulated by visiting colleague Fritz Reiner. "Thank you for a delightful evening with Beecham and Mozart," Reiner offered. Replied Sir Thomas: "Why drag in Mozart?"

For many years before he died at eighty-one, **Herbert von Karajan** was among the most sought-after conductors in the business, at one point reportedly earning more than $6 million a year. One day, went a joke popular when he was at his peak, the conductor hailed a taxi. "Where to?" asked the driver. "It doesn't matter," von Karajan answered. "I'm in demand everywhere."

Giacomo Puccini's *Gianni Schicchi* premiered in Rome, with the composer doing the podium honors. After the performance, members of the orchestra called for him to return to the stage for a bow. He held back, even as one musician came and took him by the arm. The musician was about to give in to the composer-conductor's modesty when he heard Puccini whisper, "Pull, pull!"

Serge Koussevitzky was approached after a concert by an overly dramatic woman who fell on her knees weeping at the sight of him. "Maestro," she cried, "you conducted like God!" The conductor helped the woman to her feet. "You are right, madame," he answered, beginning to sob himself. "And just think of the responsibility."

Podium Put-Downs

Teddy Roosevelt said, "Speak softly and carry a big stick." Many conductors prefer to speak loudly and carry a small baton. Those who don't speak loudly often speak sarcastically, particularly when discussing those roadblocks on the path to their musical ideals: musicians.

- Someone once recommended a soloist to Sir Thomas Beecham. Sir Thomas declined. "As a violinist," the conductor said, "he has only one defect—he can't play the violin."
- Otto Klemperer was not known to be overly generous with praise. About the most exuberant he ever got was the time he shouted, "Good!" at the end of one difficult piece. The happy orchestra burst into applause. Klemperer scowled. "Not *that* good," he sneered.
- To a young conductor, Richard Strauss once advised: "Never look at the brass. It only encourages them."
- Strauss was no fonder of a certain soprano than he was of brass sections. At a rehearsal of his opera *Elektra*, as the singer shifted into high gear, he yelled to the orchestra, "Louder! Louder! I can still hear her!"
- It doesn't happen often that a musician turns the tables and gets the best of the conductor. But musicians everywhere smile when they hear the tale of how one of their own responded to continued verbal attacks from Josef Stransky. "If you bawl me out again," the annoyed player threatened, "I'll follow your beat."

Get set

Getting into Position

Stand straight, elbows close but not touching the body. Don't bend your knees. Keep your feet approximately parallel and several inches apart—just far enough so that you can twist fully from the hips without losing your balance. The basic rule is: You can change foot position when you have to turn all the way to one side or the other, but otherwise don't move 'em. The podium isn't a dance floor.

If you insist on taking the expression *Armchair Conductor* literally, you may conduct while seated—provided you use a chair with low arms, so they don't interfere with your own arms. Actually, a chair with *no* arms is better. An eighteenth-century harpsichord bench would be nice, if you happen to have one.

The Field

The strike zone for the tip of the baton is a rough square on a vertical plane about eighteen inches in front of you, covering an area a foot and a half or so to either side of your shirt buttons, from your waist to the top of your head. The x-axis—the line along which you make left-right motions—runs across your lower ribs. The y-axis—the up-down line described by the point of the baton—runs straight up the middle of the strike zone, following a line in front of your shirt buttons.

How much of the field you use depends on what you're conducting—most importantly, how loud the music is. On occasion, when the volume or the emotion is unusually high, you might go beyond the normal limits.

DOING BUSINESS WITH THE BATON

The Basic Patterns

Nearly all the music you listen to has a recognizable pulse, or rhythm—mostly 2-beat, 3-beat, or 4-beat. The 2-beat—ONE-*two*, ONE-*two*—is the familiar rhythm of a march (LEFT-right, LEFT-right) or your heart (THUMP-thump, THUMP-thump). The 3-beat—ONE-*two-three*, ONE-*two-three*—is the same waltz rhythm you probably learned in junior high school dance class. The 4-beat—ONE-*two*-THREE-*four*, ONE-*two*-THREE-*four*—is the most common of all; you hear it in everything from "White Christmas" to Tchaikovsky's *1812 Overture*.

Standard conducting gestures are made up of vertical and lateral movements, with a distinct baton pattern for each musical pattern. Very roughly, they look like this:

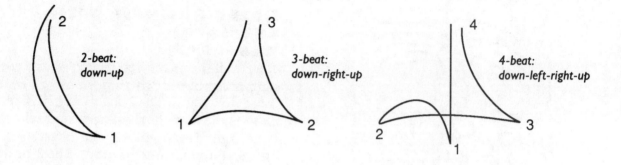

2-beat:
down-up

3-beat:
down-right-up

4-beat:
down-left-right-up

Beyond 4-beat, things get too complicated for the beginning Armchair Conductor. This book will cover only what you need, and even this you don't have to learn all at once. (Yes, there *is* a 1-beat; more about it later.)

Musicians watch the *tip* of the stick, so you'll be conducting with the tip and letting your arm follow. Think of the baton as an extension of your forearm; it's a straight line from your elbow to the point of the stick. When you follow the diagrams coming up,

trace the path with the tip. Each stroke may carry the tip just a few inches, in very soft passages, or two or three feet, in very loud or wildly expressive passages.

ANGLES AND CURVES

Music flows in different ways—sometimes snappy or sharp (like "Yankee Doodle"), sometimes smooth or even voluptuous (like your favorite love song or lullaby). When the music is snappy, it's called *staccato*

(Italian for "detached"); when the music is smooth, it's *legato* (also Italian; it means "tied together").

When the baton traces the patterns, its tip changes direction either by stopping cold and bouncing off each point in the diagram, with a flick of the wrist (in the case of staccato music) or by rolling through a broad curve, with more forearm movement (when the passage is legato). There are multitudes of possible variations; we offer two for each basic rhythm—an angular staccato and a curvy legato. In each case, the underlying geometry is the same. With a little experience, you'll be able to feel from the music how straight or rounded your patterns should be.

For staccato moves, use a crisp, whip-cracking motion. To conduct legato, keep your motions fluid, even silky.

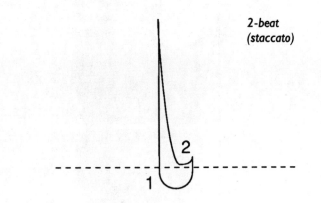

2-beat
(staccato)

2
1

2-BEAT

ONE-*two*, ONE-*two*. Although commonly thought of as march time, the 2-beat is found in a variety of music, such as "London Bridge," Jean-Joseph Mouret's "Fanfare for the King's Supper" (the theme from *Masterpiece Theatre*), the overture to Jacques Offenbach's *Orpheus in the Underworld* ("Cancan Music"), "Flight of the Bumblebee," the bridal chorus from Wagner's *Lohengrin* ("Here Comes the Bride"), and the *William Tell Overture*.

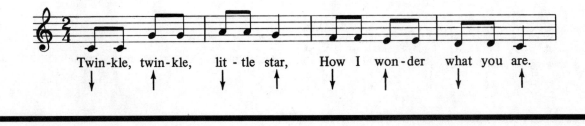

"Twinkle, Twinkle, Little Star" ("The Alphabet Song") (staccato)

Twin-kle, twin-kle, lit-tle star, How I won-der what you are.

The staccato 2-beat (down-up, down-up) drops to just below the *x*-axis, hooks slightly to the right, like a backward J, stops cold, and shoots back up to the starting point. Keep the hook small, but make sure it's a real hook; don't just beat straight down-up. The action should be as if you're picking a bit of lint with the tip of the baton.

Most 2-beat music is staccato, but for the rare legato piece, the pattern makes a broad backward-J curve, regains half its height, then smoothly scoops leftward and back up.

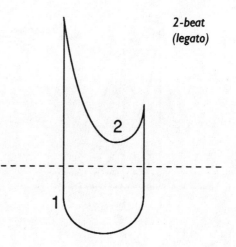

2-beat
(legato)

"Swing Low, Sweet Chariot" (legato)

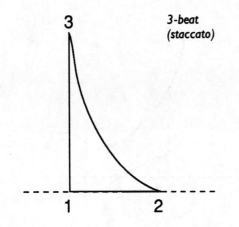

3

3-beat
(staccato)

1   2

3-BEAT

ONE-*two-three*, ONE-*two-three*. It's not only a waltz—it's a mazurka, it's the third movement of most of Haydn's 104 symphonies, it's any music that fits over a background of OOM-pah-pah, OOM-pah-pah. There's "Greensleeves," the first movement of Beethoven's *Eroica* Symphony (No. 3), the third movement of Tchaikovsky's Fifth Symphony, the first movement of Schubert's *Unfinished* Symphony (No. 8), Brahms's

"East Side, West Side" ("Sidewalks of New York") (staccato)

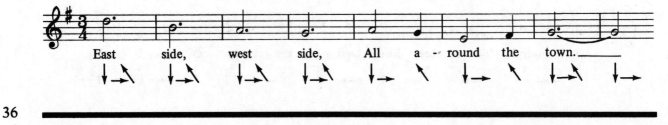

East   side,   west   side,   All   a - round   the   town.

"Lullaby," and "On Top of Old Smoky."

In 3-beat, the baton tip roughly traces a right triangle: down-right-up, down-right-up, with "up" being back along the hypotenuse to the start. In the staccato mode, simply curve the hypotenuse a bit. In legato, the downbeat is straight, and then the line loops and curves continuously until it loops around to begin the descent again; however much looping goes on, the basic shape is still a right triangle.

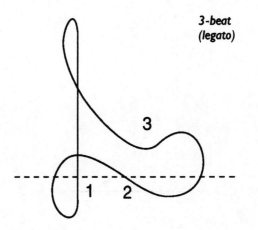

3-beat
(legato)

"America" ("God Save the Queen") (legato)

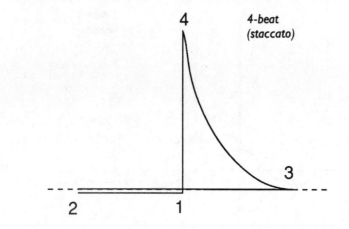

4-beat
(staccato)

4-BEAT

ONE-*two*-THREE-*four*, ONE-*two*-THREE-*four*. (If the tempo is so fast that you want to rest your arm awhile, you can beat a slow 2 instead of a fast 4.) Count it out to pieces like "Adeste Fideles," the main theme of "Stars and Stripes Forever" ("Be Kind to Your Web-Footed Friends"), the "Anvil Chorus" from Verdi's *Il Trovatore*, the finale of Brahms's First Symphony, and "When the Saints Go Marching In."

"Hallelujah Chorus" from Handel's Messiah (staccato)

Hal - le - lu - jah!   Hal - le - lu - jah!   Hal-le - lu-jah!   Hal-le-lu-jah!   Hal - le - lu-jah!

The underlying pattern of 4-beat is down-left-right-up, down-left-right-up. The staccato diagram shows most clearly how the third beat retraces the path of the second, overshooting the *y*-axis before stopping, reversing, and scooping up to the starting point. The legato diagram only *looks* complicated; it's just the same pattern with the loops and rounded corners necessary to keep the music flowing. Try it a few times; you'll catch on.

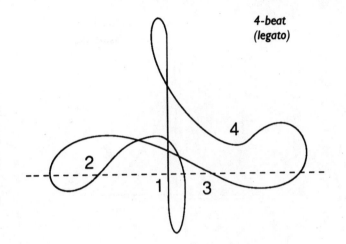

4-beat
(legato)

"Old Folks at Home" (legato)

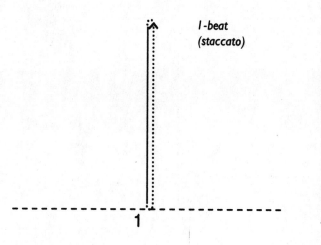

1-beat
(staccato)

1

1-BEAT

ONE, ONE, ONE, ONE. There isn't much music written in 1-beat, but the pattern has a good use. What do you do when a piece of music is just too fast to mark every beat with your baton, as in many scherzo movements of symphonies and other very fast passages? The conductor's solution—*your* solution—is to pretend they're in 1-beat.

A few familiar cases are "Comin' 'Round the Mountain," "Cielito Lindo" ("Ay, Ay, Ay, Ay") and the scherzos from Mendelssohn's

"Take Me Out to the Ball Game" (staccato)

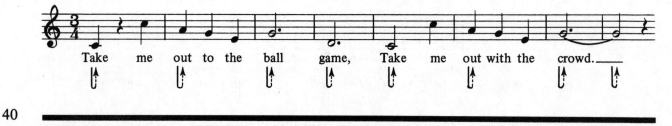

Take me out to the ball game, Take me out with the crowd.____

A Midsummer Night's Dream and
Beethoven's Third and Ninth symphonies.
Many popular waltzes go best in 1.

Don't think the 1-beat pattern is the same
as the 2-beat. It's quite different. The 2-beat
is down-up—two distinct strokes separated
by a pause. The 1-beat is a *single* motion
that speeds up as it drops, bounces back,
and slows as it heads for the starting place;
when it gets there, it does an instantaneous
reversal and heads down for the next beat.
In the staccato mode, the stroke resembles a
cigar; for legato, a misshapen pear.

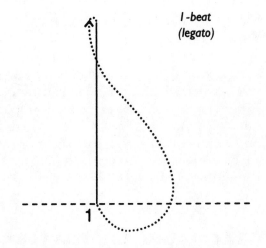

1-beat
(legato)

1

"Daisy, Daisy" ("Bicycle Built for Two") (legato)

41

WHEN THE GOING GETS TOUGH

You can deal with some of the more complex rhythms by using the short division you learned in third grade. For instance, "Silent Night," as written, is an example of a 6-beat; conduct it as a slow 3-beat and no one will be the wiser. As for 5-beat or other such complexities, do yourself a favor: Find something else to conduct.

PRACTICING THE PATTERNS

As you practice the patterns—even as you beat time with recorded music—count to yourself: "ONE-*two*, ONE-*two* . . . ." If you're practicing very slow tempos (which are harder to beat smoothly than medium speeds), try a nice, even "ONE-*and-two-and* . . . ." Such silent counting is the mental equivalent of foot tapping; it helps.

PAY NO ATTENTION TO THIS MAN! Sir Adrian Boult, one of England's premier conductors for much of this century, was also author of a respected handbook of conducting technique. Here, he grasps the bulb by his fingertips, inadvertently demonstrating the wrong way to hold a baton.

Go!

MAESTRO, IF YOU PLEASE

First, hold your baton in the neutral position, or position of attention. Here's how:

- With the point of the baton in front of you, move your elbow about 45° out to the side and slightly forward. (Remember to bring it back closer to the body as soon as you start the music.)
- Keep your forearm more or less parallel to the floor.
- Place the tip of the baton at a spot several inches right of center, about chin height.

In calling for attention, it's common to raise the left hand to mirror the baton. For control of the wrist, bring the tips of the thumb and index finger together (forming a flattened oval), but don't clench your hand.

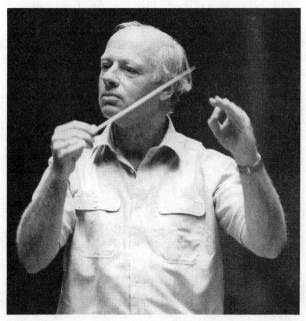

Bernard Haitink: "All set?"

STARTING ON 1

The simplest starts to execute are those in which the first note falls on the first beat—the ONE. Here's how to handle them:

No counting off à la Lawrence Welk ("An' a-one, an' a-two . . . "). Start the music with a single preparatory beat, beginning at the attention position. The preparatory beat is the last stroke of whichever diagram you'll be following, the one that curves up:

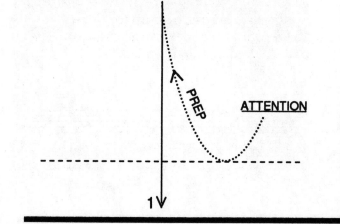

From the way a conductor makes this single gesture, eighty to a hundred musicians instantly surmise how to play the notes that follow. The speed of the baton on this one stroke tells them how fast to play, because the preparatory beat is executed strictly in tempo. The size and intensity of the stroke tell them how loud to play. The timing of the stroke makes them begin simultaneously.

Boy, is conducting complicated!

But calm down. For the Armchair Conductor there's no question of controlling a hundred musicians. In fact, the music controls you. But that makes your job easy. Here's how *you* "start" the music:

Put on a familiar recording*—something you can count in four. From the neutral position, inhale and swing through a *four* and keep the baton at the top. Hold your breath. When the music starts, play catch-up by instantly dropping the stick in the ONE of ONE-*two*-THREE-*four*, exhaling as you go, and heading into the pattern you've memorized. With a very little practice, you can learn to fake-start an orchestra and get into a smooth movement within a beat or two.

For starters, let the left hand mirror the baton hand, coming up from the left and then dropping with the baton. Let your left hand duplicate the baton's moves in mirror image for a while, and then drop out. (*Mirror image:* When the baton goes up and down, the left hand goes up and down; when the baton goes left, the left hand goes right; when the baton goes right, the left hand goes left.)

*The advent of the CD has hurt the Loyal Order of Armchair Conductors. Vinyl discs (remember vinyl discs?) made it easy to fake-start your favorite symphony: Just memorize the snaps and pops and hisses on the opening grooves and you knew when to give the preparatory beat and come in with authority. With CDs, those clues are gone. You can hardly conduct staring at the digital display. Instead, a higher degree of fakery is required.

STARTING ON 2, 3, OR 4 (A LITTLE TOUGHER)

Same principle: Give, as a preparatory beat, the beat preceding the one the music starts on in the pattern. As an example, try "Happy Birthday." It's a 3-beat song and starts with "Happy . . ." on the third beat. The preparatory beat, therefore, is 2 in the ONE-*two*-*three* pattern: a stroke to the right.

To start the song, silently count (in tempo) "ONE-*two*-*three*, ONE—" then stroke the preparatory *two* across, beat up for *three* ("Happy"), down to start the ONE-*two*-*three* pattern, and on into the piece:

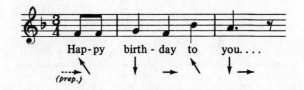

TEMPO, TEMPO

Q. How fast should you beat time?

A. As fast as the recording you're conducting. (As an Armchair Conductor, you don't have to worry about fast, slow, or in between; tempos are set for you.)

A conductor who presides over real live musicians, on the other hand, has decisions to make. When a composer scores a work with a metronome* marking—so many beats per minute—there's no room for dispute. But often, musical direction is given not in numbers but in words, which are subject to interpretation.

Some conductors are incredibly sensitive to the speed of their music. Herbert von Karajan used to say that yoga practice made him unusually aware of his own heartbeat. When you conduct a piece at your own pulse rate, he told one interviewer, "your whole body makes music." He mentioned a time he took some tapes from a recording session to his home in St. Moritz, Switzerland, and found they sounded wrong. "Then I realized," he said. "In St. Moritz you are higher, and your heartbeat is faster."

Conductors love to debate any question of tempo. "I don't care," William Steinberg once grumped. "I still prefer my own wrong tempi to the wrong tempi of my colleagues." Conductors take tempos so seriously that they call them "tempi."

*Metronome: a little box that sits and goes "tick-tock," just like an old pendulum clock, at whatever speed you set it. Not so many years ago, a conductor who didn't have a metronome handy could use a wristwatch. The standard old-style watch movement produced 300 ticks a minute, so counting every fifth tick, for example, gave a speed of 60 beats a minute. Today's quartz watches, unfortunately, don't tick.

Household Hint

Egg timer broken? Use this handy substitute timing method from Sir John Barbirolli, as he offered it to a radio audience during a BBC talk show:

"I always have a boiled egg, a three-minute egg. Do you know how I time it? I bring it to the boil and then conduct the Overture to *The Marriage of Figaro*. Three minutes exactly."

GIVING CUES

For the Armchair Conductor, giving cues is almost as important as it is for the real-life conductor. It isn't that there are musicians in danger of missing a big entrance. It's that giving cues makes you look like you're in charge.

The conductor prepares the musicians with a glance several seconds ahead of time, then gives cues *precisely on the beat of the*

Fritz Reiner:
"You! Now!"

entrance. There are four common ways of cuing, here presented in order of increasing boldness:

- Properly timed eye contact can gently say, "Now."
- A nod says the same thing more strongly.
- Without disturbing the pattern being traced, the baton directed toward a player or section is an even more direct cue.
- The most direct: the *left* index finger is held up, slightly bent, and, at the appropriate time, gently but firmly moved in mirror imitation of the baton's movement. (Never give a finger cue with a rigid finger, which could be interpreted as being accusatory; musicians are *so* sensitive.) For a dramatic cue on a *really* big downbeat entrance, make a fist, knuckles up, and drop it smartly as the baton falls.

A Cue Story

Bruno Walter once faced a new tenor whose musicianship unfortunately didn't match his splendid vocal equipment. At rehearsal after rehearsal, the newcomer consistently missed a certain key entrance. At length, Walter suggested that at the performance the singer should keep his eyes glued to the podium, and when the moment arrived, he would cue him heavily with his left hand. Evening came. The curtain rose. The opera went along splendidly. At the appointed time, Walter raised his hand and dropped his finger. A bewildered cry was heard from the tenor: "Who, me?"

Cuing is one area that can't be faked. If you know when the big brass entrance comes, you can cue the section and you'll look great. But cue even one beat off and you can look supremely foolish. That's why you should work with recorded music you know well. (After two or three tries at Armchair Conducting a piece, you'll know it a lot better than before—a reward for hard work.)

For cuing practice, get four friends to help. Line them up and conduct a round of "Frère Jacques." Cue each singer in turn. Join in and sing yourself, if you like. Now try "Row, Row, Row Your Boat."

VOLUME CONTROL

The baton is the orchestra's chief volume control: the bigger the motion, the bigger the sound. For music that's *forte* (loud), the baton should trace a larger version of the pattern; for music that's *piano* (soft), a small version. *Piano* may also be called for by pulling the arms in near the body, which naturally restricts arm movements to a small size. Generally, for small, quiet beats, let your wrist do the work; for medium-sized, moderately soft beats, the wrist and forearm together do the job. Only during very large beats, indicating *fortissimo*—very loud—should the upper arm go to work.

The left hand, too, as noted, can have something to say about how loud the music is: a dribbling motion (palm down, gently bobbing) for softer, the reverse (palm up) for louder. To the Armchair Conductor, of course, the trick is that the instant you hear

Roger Norrington: "Shhh!"

James Levine: "Gimme more!"

the music getting louder, up goes the palm. If the volume drops, turn the palm down.

Most critics and instructors frown on conductors who use their bodies to demand extremes of volume: nearly leaping in the air to bring on a triple-*forte* and doing deep knee-bends to hush the orchestra into a triple-*piano*. But it does work, and in the privacy of your own home, why not? Just limit such dramatics to true extremes or you'll quickly debase the currency.

Sir John Barbirolli: "I said, 'Easy!'"

SPECIALTY SIGNALS

You won't find symphonic conductors using left-hand signals, but leaders of show pit bands, jazz and studio groups, school bands, and all kinds of amateur ensembles commonly use a roster of reminders such as:

- two, three, or four fingers in the air = time change coming (to 2, 3, or 4 beats);
- small repeated circles with index finger = repeat coming;
- raised fist = take the ending (ignore the written repeat, or watch for a cutoff signal);
- finger to head = *da capo* (go back to the beginning);
- finger drawn across throat = don't forget that we agreed to cut a part from the written score—watch for the marked changes.

STOP THE MUSIC!

Here's where you can shine: A conductor looks and feels most like a conductor during a good, ride-'em-home ending. (Corollary: Watch out! Mess up a big finish and you have slipped on a musical banana peel. Hans Richter knew what he was talking about when he said, "The hardest thing in the world is to start an orchestra. The next hardest is to stop it.")

The secret for avoiding embarrassment is no secret: Prepare. Know the music; know when and how it ends. If you can sing the ending without a mistake, you can conduct it—as long as you know the moves that fit.

A piece that just finishes what it's doing and stops—in tempo, according to rhythm, as you'd expect—is no problem to end. Just finish off the last beat with a snappy rebound to the top of the field. At the same time, do the mirror image of that move with your left hand. Hold right there for a second or two and drop both hands. If you can, make that last move a downbeat instead of whatever other stroke the last note falls on. That way, your rebound can bring both hands up to top-of-head level, always an impressive place to finish.

There are, however, bigger endings that are much more impressive to bring off. They come in two basic categories, which we can call *chop-chop-chop* and *hold-and-cut*.

By chop-chop-chop we mean any ending that consists of one or more short blasts, whether it be a single kicker in perfect rhythm or several big chords. A hold-and-cut finishes on a note that sounds, unchanging, for as long as the conductor keeps his baton up. The finale of Beethoven's Fifth Symphony combines both: a long, long buildup capped by six chopping C-major chords plus a long hold-

and-cut. The ending of the same composer's Eighth Symphony is even more of a showcase for the Armchair Conductor. Or try the *1812 Overture* or *Marche Slav* of Tchaikovsky, the *Roman Carnival* Overture of Berlioz, or Gershwin's *American in Paris*. But you probably have your own favorite happy endings.

To execute a chop-chop-chop ending, just slash away in time to the music, preferably following the pattern you've been tracing, except that your strokes may be bigger and more dramatic, if the music is more intense. Wherever you are in the pattern, make the last stroke a huge downbeat and immediately rebound high. Mirror the final stroke with your left hand and hold both hands up a few seconds before dropping your arms (to tumultuous applause).

For a final hold-and-cut, rebound high, keep the baton up for as long as the last note sounds, and end with a flourish. This requires a bit more knowledge. . . .

PAUSES AND CUTOFFS

During a *fermata*, or hold (⌒ in musical notation), the baton stops dead about halfway through the stroke. Here, the left hand often comes in to indicate volume: If the note fades, the left hand is turned palm down, sometimes lowered as well. If the note is to remain loud, the left hand goes palm up; shake the hand close to the body for even more sound.

If the music continues immediately after the hold, keep the baton in place as long as the hold lasts; continue with the rest of the stroke, in tempo, as prep for the next beat; then go on. Try, for example, the third line of "Happy Birthday," which traditionally ends with a hold on the last syllable of the celebrant's name:

Hap-py birth-day dear Lud-wi-i-ig, Hap-py birth-day. . .

(prep.)

Frequently, a hold finishes with a cutoff—either before going on or at the end of a piece. The cutoff flourish most often used is made by drawing the baton tip in a rapidly accelerating counterclockwise spiral, tightly curling into a final flick:

If the music continues after hold-and-cut, finish the beat you were on as a preparatory beat for the continuation: half-stroke, hold, spiral cutoff, finish stroke, continue the pattern. If the hold-and-cut comes at the end of a passage, the left hand can mirror the cutoff, making a fast *clockwise* spiral with the index finger extended. This kind of mimicry isn't a must, but with endings, as with beginnings, it's effective.

Back to "Happy Birthday": The last line is usually sung with a schmaltzy *ritardando*—slowing—and a hold on the final "you-u-u." Bounce the baton back to the top on the final downbeat, pause, and do your counterclockwise cutoff starting from about one o'clock. Your left hand can copy the baton's final five strokes, but while the baton holds

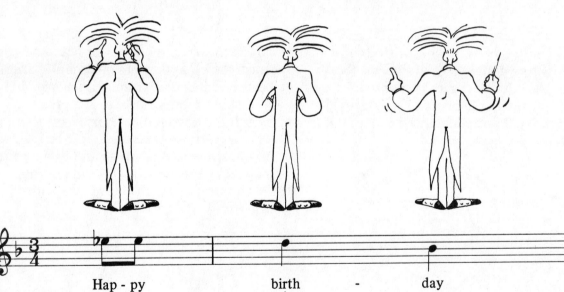

Hap - py   birth - day

the last note the left hand quickly turns over to the palm-up position, shaking slightly to indicate a request to keep the volume up. To finish, the baton and left hand do the sharp spiral cutoff move together—the baton counterclockwise, the left hand, suddenly clenched with index finger extended, clockwise. Nice job.

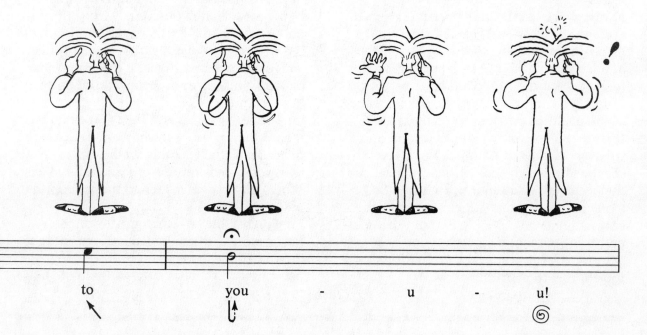

to   you -   u -   u!

Concerto for Solo Instrument and Armchair Conductor

If you Armchair-Conduct a piece with a soloist, remember that the conductor always works to the orchestra but keeps an eye on the soloist. So give an occasional glance over your left shoulder, like a left-handed pitcher in a stretch position trying to pick a runner off second base.

During a cadenza (when the soloist shows off unaccompanied), don't conduct at all. During the orchestra's silence, stand unobtrusively with your baton down. A few seconds before the end of the cadenza, call the orchestra to attention; an imperious look can be effective. It helps to know the cadenza, but if you don't, in most classical and some romantic concertos you need only wait for the big trill-and-turn that signals the ending; then dive back in.

How to Fake with Style

What if you want to conduct music you don't know? You don't immediately recognize the pattern of beats. Now what?

Put on your best pretend-authority face. Using a small, quiet motion, with your wrist only, start making gentle vertical ovals, accenting what sounds like the first beat. In effect, you're taking it as a 1-beat. If the tempo is slow enough, you can even make an oval on every beat. Before long, you'll probably detect a pattern of accented beats. When you catch on, make a bigger oval on what you hear as the pulse beat, smaller ovals on the others. That way, you avoid committing yourself too early. When you're sure, switch to the appropriate pattern.

If you lose the beat during an Armchair Performance, the same trick can be pulled out of storage to help you find your way back: just make ovals until you find the pulse.

Putting it all together

Working as a Team: Left and Right

An Armchair Conductor with a little experience can usually fake the right hand's job pretty well. It's the left hand that can cause problems. Perhaps the most noticeable mark of an amateur conductor is not knowing what to do with the left hand.

The tendency is to let the left arm hang limp at the side or continuously mirror the baton. Working conductors know how to perform many functions with the left hand, but they generally use it sparingly; during off times, it rests comfortably by the body. Mirroring the baton hand is properly done when there's something to clarify or emphasize in the music. When there's a sudden change in volume or in tempo, for example,

James DePreist,
left hand at the ready

it's okay to play copycat. Otherwise, constant duplication makes the conductor look unnecessarily active, which is why among musicians it's sneeringly called "swimming."

Richard Strauss used to advise jamming the left hand into the coat pocket during quiet times, but you'd be better advised to hold it relaxed in front of your waist, where it's ready to jump in when needed. Now and then, for just a few moments, you may pat the air with your left hand on each stressed beat, as a rhythm reinforcer (it also gives the hand something to do). This is a particularly reassuring trick to use while Armchair-Conducting music you don't know well—the long-forgotten recording or the unfamiliar but appealing piece being played on the radio.

Two-Hand Training

These exercises, done faithfully, will help you get used to moving your hands independently:

- Using forearms only, move one hand up and down while the other draws a circle of medium size in front of the body; change hands.
- Beat a moderate-tempo 4-beat pattern with the right hand and practice introducing an occasional left-hand gesture, such as a cue to one side or the other or calling for louder and softer playing.
- Pat your head with one hand while you rub your stomach with the other.
- If you can't do any of the above, see if you can walk and chew gum at the same time.

How to Get to Carnegie Hall

If you aspire to a full symphonic repertory, the best pieces to practice, practice, practice are works by Bach, Vivaldi, or other composers of the baroque period. From the Armchair Conductor's point of view, they are thankfully free of messy tempo changes: You get started, you keep going, you stop. They're perfect for putting your right hand into automatic and practicing your left-hand gestures and body moves. An evening or two working with a recording of "The Four Seasons" and cuing the trumpet in the Brandenburg Concerto No. 2, and you're on your way to Mahler.

If you get to the point in baroque practice where things seem to be going too smoothly and there isn't much to do, invent problems that require action. Turn half-profile to the right, bring in your left hand to emphasize the beat, and glare at the cellos. If you like the idea of conducting rehearsals, you could also stop the music and lecture the entire cello section on the importance of precision, because cellos are the foundation of the orchestra, and on and on. . . . (Don't get too carried away with the sound of your own voice. One great German maestro once did just that at a rehearsal, droning on about the composer's true meaning and the inter-relationship of art and civilization. At last, a horn player interrupted. "Just tell us," he demanded, "whether you want us to play loud or soft.")

Making your own music while you conduct—singing, humming, or whistling—can be good for practice too. Conducting live music—even self-made—is closer to the real experience than following a recording. But unless you have an especially vivid imagination, it rarely sounds as good.

THE ARMCHAIR CONDUCTOR'S FIVE FAVORITE FLICKS

WHAT	WHO	WHY
Fantasia	Leopold Stokowski	Mickey conducting,* Mickey shaking Stoki's hand
Unfaithfully Yours	Your choice: Rex Harrison (1948) or Dudley Moore ('83 remake)	Lots of baton action — the conductor's the leading role
Once More with Feeling	Yul Brynner	The King conducts
Casablanca	Bogie and Bergman	Victor Laszlo beating time as Rick's band drowns out the Nazi anthem with "La Marseillaise"
A Night at the Opera	The Marxes	Harpo dueling the conductor, violin bow versus baton

*A major first for rodent conductors. Mick conducts batonless, using just his gloved four-fingered hands. Imagine how great he'd have been if he'd had *five* fingers on each hand.

*Harpo and Chico in
A Night at
the Opera*

FIELD WORK

Front-and-center: best seats in the house, right? Wrong.

For theater tickets, perhaps. But at a concert, you want to see the conductor's hands at work, not that part of the anatomy you'd see from the middle of the house.

So sit front row, but far left or far right. Go with a friend who's also an Armchair Conductor and buy seats on opposite sides of the house; switch halfway through the evening and each of you will have a good look from both angles.

On field trips, don't be disturbed or frustrated if you don't immediately recognize every move the conductor makes. This book is teaching you the basic language; most conductors speak with a very fancy vocabulary. (Want to see a conductor who makes mostly nice, basic moves? Go to a junior high school band concert.)

How to Conduct Beethoven's Fifth Symphony

Da da da daaa! Da da da daaaaa!____

Three Gs and an E flat, three Fs and a D—the most famous eight notes in the symphonic literature. If you're going to conduct, you just *have* to conduct Beethoven's Fifth.

At least the beginning.

Now, despite its simple, hummable quality, Beethoven's "fate knocking at the door" theme is one of the most dangerous openings to conduct. Seasoned pros (including, among others, Toscanini) have presided over fiascos starting the piece. Oscar Levant may have had the right idea when he was asked, "How would *you* conduct the Beethoven Fifth?" Said Levant: "I'd skip the first four bars."

Well, you don't have to.

You will have a recording that makes no errors. The performance will be superb, guaranteed. All you have to do is match it.

Although Beethoven wrote it in 2-beat, the passage is most often played so fast you should conduct it as a 1-beat. Remember the 1-beat pattern? You make a fast drop and a quick reverse, slowing as you reach top again.

Here's the blow-by-blow:

- Start the recording and raise your baton high. You can't know from a recording when the invisible conductor gives the downbeat, so you're going to skip the first beat and fake your way into the piece.
- Listen for the *da da da*. When you hear them, drop the baton for the *daaa*; with a few practices, you'll be able to hit bottom just at the moment it sounds. Immediately rebound, as you do in any 1-beat pattern.
- At the top, hold and execute a spiral cutoff in time with the orchestra; learn when to end it by counting silently to your recording a couple of times.
- There'll be no time to spare after the cutoff: you need to make *two* consecutive cigar shapes—immediately. The goal is to hit down the first time just before the second *da da da*; the second drop of the baton should hit precisely *on* the final *daaaaa*, then rebound, hold, and cut; again, listen to your recording ahead of time to learn how long the *daaaaa* lasts.

Let the left hand join on the holds and cutoffs, but otherwise keep it out of the way. You have enough to worry about.

It may take six or eight tries, but with perseverance you *will* be able to time the whole thing right. If you really have trouble, dig out an old recording of the Fifth from the days when conductors took the opening so slowly that you can conduct each note individually:

Da . . . da . . . da . . . daaa!

HOW TO SNATCH VICTORY

It's bound to happen: You signal a big cutoff and the music keeps playing, or the music comes to a halt and you keep on flapping. What a mess!

But wait! Don't apologize, don't make excuses, don't crawl under a table. The Armchair Conductor should be skilled at bluffing through such mishaps. You may lack the Big League Conductor's schooling and experience, not to mention raw talent. But even the Armchair Conductor—*especially* the Armchair Conductor—must perform with total confidence. Criticism is not to be taken lightly. In fact, criticism is not to be taken at all. Never forget: In your living room, in your car, in your fantasies, *you* are the maestro.

If some unthinking observer breaches etiquette by criticizing or smirking at your efforts, do not resort to the Armchair

Conductor's instinctive responses, which include comebacks like:

- "All right, so I'm *not* Esa-Pekka Salonen."
- "Let's see you do better, cello-head!"
- "Oh, yeah?"

Instead, you might try one of these elementary ploys:

- Stop the recording, scowl at the orchestra, and say sternly, "Take it from the top—and let's get it right this time!"
- Look knowingly at your audience, shake your head, and say, "I warned them about that in rehearsal."

And remember . . .

The Conductor Is Always Right

Sir Thomas Beecham, beginning a rehearsal for a guest appearance, halted the music and called out, "First trombone—too loud!"

"But, Sir Thomas," piped up a flute player, "the first trombonist hasn't arrived yet."

Beecham didn't miss a beat. "Well, then," he countered, raising his baton to resume the music making, "when he does get here, tell him he's playing too loud."

Role Models

From Out of the Past

Even the most content of Armchair Conductors may daydream of life beyond the armchair: the power and glory of leading a real orchestra and being addressed as "Maestro," not to mention the lucrative recording contracts and first-class airline seats. But the dream is usually hazy. To fine-tune it, you need a role model—someone whose style, attitude, abilities, or, indeed, deficits strike a chord in harmony, as it were, with you and your dreams.

Here are some legendary greats who may provide inspiration. Brought to you as a public service.

Mr. Show Biz: Louis Antoine Jullien

Before there was Elvis or Liberace, there was Louis Antoine Jullien. A Frenchman who made it big in England in the middle 1800s, he turned himself into the first matinee idol of the music world by wearing the fanciest duds he could find, reading scores from a gilt music stand, and waving a long jeweled baton decorated with gold rings and gold serpents with diamonds in their heads. Before the first downbeat, an assistant handed him white gloves on a silver tray, and when his work was done he sank into a velvet-covered chair, flamboyantly wiping his brow with a silk handkerchief. He often played outdoors for the masses, spicing up performances with cannon, fireworks, and "the biggest drums in the world."

Circus man P. T. Barnum brought the Louie Jullien Show to the States, where at one concert he performed a piece called "Fireman's Quadrille" with an orchestra, two brass bands, and three companies of firemen, who rushed and clanged into the hall with their hoses.

Jullien died at age forty-eight, in a home for the insane.

Temperamental Genius:
Arturo Toscanini

Toscanini wasn't the only high-strung genius around, but because the combination of a colossal talent and radio made him the chief musical legend of the mid-twentieth century, his name—even decades after his death—seems synonymous with that character type. Toscanini's passion was such that he was frequently heard humming and singing accompaniment to his orchestra—even on records. Many tales are told about his explosiveness. Indeed, his treatment of the players—who nonetheless rarely questioned his musical genius—was so abusive that when his young grand-daughter visited a rehearsal one day she asked, logically, "Why don't the musicians yell back at Grandfather?"

At rehearsals, the maestro often found a physical outlet: more than once, he dug his hands into his

drawing by Enrico Caruso

jacket pockets so violently that he ripped them. He was once sued by a violinist whose eye got in the way of his baton, which had become airborne. His most frequent response to frustration was to snap his baton in two. At one less-than-happy rehearsal, he was using a flexible stick that bent but refused to break. Toscanini pulled a handkerchief from his pocket and tried to rip it; he couldn't. Finally, puffing and growing ever redder, he flung off his jacket and tore it to shreds. "Now," he said, with a new air of calmness, "from the beginning."

And there was the occasion—perhaps the most celebrated in the oral tradition of the music world—on which Toscanini became enraged at a certain musician. After an especially vicious dressing down, he sent the hapless fellow to the showers. As the musician passed the podium, he snarled a popular two-word invective. Toscanini waved him away. "No, no!" he shot back. "Too late to apologize!"

Gentleman Conductor: Pierre Monteux

Short and dapper, with coal-black hair he insisted was natural and a thick mustache that led Alexander Woollcott to describe him as "right out of Grover

Cleveland's Cabinet," Pierre Monteux was often compared to an old-fashioned French bandmaster. A perfect role model for the Armchair Conductor with a taste for the refined.

The only time the elegant Frenchman ever ruffled any feathers was when he led the historic premiere of Igor Stravinsky's *The Rite of Spring*, a work so revolutionary for its time that it sparked fistfights in the

audience. Years later, as a mentor of many young conductors, he compiled a list of "dos and don'ts" that included:

- Stand straight even if you are tall.
- Be dignified from the time you come onstage.
- Don't be disrespectful of your players (no swearing).

When a young André Previn began to imitate the energetic and theatrical moves of Leonard Bernstein, Monteux counseled: "Dear boy, before you try to impress the ladies in the mezzanine, make sure that the horns come in."

Talented Rich Kid:
Sir Thomas Beecham

When Beecham's parents told him, "Tommy—time to practice!" they meant with a full orchestra or opera company hired for the occasion. Beecham's father—also a Sir—had more pounds than he knew what to do with, from a business that made Beecham's Little Liver Pills and Beecham's Powder. It may be too late for you to do anything about your own inheritance, but if you happen to fit the mold, you could have fun emulating Beecham.

No tormented, antisocial musical genius, he was comfortable living the life of a man of property and privilege, a bon vivant, a darling of England's high society. Books were compiled of the hundreds of his insults and general witticisms that made the rounds. From his loose lip it was obvious that he was a man who didn't have to work for a living. He once dismissed the entire field of conducting in one short quip: "It's easy. All you have to do is waggle a stick."

71

He was the only conductor ever to have a real career on the big screen: four pictures, including a starring role with Deanna Durbin in *100 Men and a Girl* and, of course, his still celebrated tour-de-force appearance in Disney's *Fantasia*.

In true Hollywood fashion, Stoki shaved five years off his age; music was important, but image no less so. He was born in London but insisted he was of Eastern European birth and spoke with a mysterious, indeterminate accent. As conductor of the Philadelphia Symphony, Stokowski abandoned his baton and ordered the house lights at the Academy of Music repositioned, with new spotlights to focus on his sensuous, long-fingered hands and on his profile and flowing white mane. He had, it was said, liaisons by the dozen, including flings with Greta Garbo (the facts of which are still in dispute) and Gloria Vanderbilt (who became his third wife).

Once, a fan brought up his role in *Fantasia*, referring to the famous scene in which the maestro, on the podium, stoops to greet the world's most famous rodent. "You're the only man I know who shook hands with Mickey Mouse," the fan gushed. "No, no, no," Stoki corrected sternly. "*He* shook hands with *me*."

**Movie Star:
Leopold
Stokowski**

The Bad Luck Kid: Otto Klemperer

For those whose feet always seem to find where the dog stopped, there is Otto Klemperer, a hulking, deadly serious leader of whom a musician once said, "Two hours with Klemperer is like two hours in church."

- In 1933, he fell off a podium and landed on his head; he suffered headaches for the rest of his life and brain surgery left him partly paralyzed.
- In 1940, he spent time in a rest home, reportedly for a mental breakdown.
- In 1951, he fell from an airport landing ramp and broke his right thighbone.
- In 1959, he set fire to himself while smoking in bed and was seriously burned.
- In 1966, he fell and broke his hip.

Klemperer did not wave a baton to beat time; he used his clenched fist.

Who could blame him?

Cold and Spicy: Fritz Reiner

He looked like Bela Lugosi's brother. He acted the way you'd expect Bela Lugosi's brother to act.

Reiner was a master technician whose tiny baton beat, exercised with the controlled moves of an eye surgeon, was scarcely visible from the second row of violins. His ear could—it was said—hear and locate a wrong bowing even with his back turned. But memories of his musical gifts almost take a backseat to tales of his ability to inspire fear in musicians with a minimum of effort. An arched eyebrow would radiate contempt for a flat flutist, a curled lip would reveal a bottomless crevasse of condescension for a wayward cellist.

At the Cleveland Orchestra, the musicians' union complained about his treatment of its members. But Reiner didn't stop—he just changed his tune a little. When one player fouled up at a rehearsal, the only partially reformed maestro didn't yell, curse, or question the man's lineage. He dipped into his bag of sarcasm. "This morning I found a hole in my shoe," he told the musician. "I didn't know where to take it to be repaired. Now I know."

The Perfectionist: George Szell

There are, in this world, those who just do things and those who do things *right*—always. And the perfectionist personality suffers nothing less than perfection from others as well. Thus it's no surprise that George Szell was known to correct his wife's whistling.

As long as you're going to whistle, you ought to get the tempo and the pitch right.

Celebrity Spiritualist:
Herbert von Karajan

He was a Zen Buddhist who practiced yoga, a conductor who believed fervently that to conduct meant to become part of the music. The baton, the arm, even the body of a conductor, he used to say, are there merely to transmit the conductor's inner vision. Tie his arm to his body, he boasted, and he could still make an orchestra feel what he wanted. He conducted with his eyes closed because, he said, it helped relax the musicians.

But the well-traveled maestro (nickname: the General Music Director of Europe) was also a charismatic, fast-living celebrity who rehearsed in turtlenecks and Adidas, skied at his St. Moritz vacation home, piloted a Learjet and a Falcon 10, and was said to have talked his way into the cockpit of the Concorde for a try at the controls. Best proof of his celebrity status was the perk granted by his hometown city of Salzburg, Austria, host of the famous music festival. During festival time each year, a host of visiting music lovers made the streets nearly impassible. Salzburg's famous native son, whose stable of cars included a gull-wing Mercedes 300SL, was the only person allowed to drive in the bus lanes.

The Exercist: Leonard Bernstein

Are you an inspired musical powerhouse with a brilliant sense of the dramatic and an insatiable taste for the most powerful emotions? Are you a weekend athlete looking for an intense fitness routine? Then follow the Technique According to Lenny, which includes such moves as:

- thrusting your baton like a musical musketeer in a duel to subdue the score;
- grasping the stick in a two-hand grip suitable for drilling a vicious return-of-serve on the tennis court;
- leaping high enough to dunk a *fortissimo* and twisting and turning like an overactive aerobics instructor.

The "Lenny Dance" (his own name for it) was a symphony of jumps, whirls, swivels, and thrusts, often accompanied by singing or grunting. Yet he could cut all motion dead, shut his eyes, and rock his head back and forth with arms motionless for seconds—even minutes—of music.

Small wonder that the acid-tongued Oscar Levant once remarked that Bernstein "uses music as an accompaniment to his conducting."

THE CONTEMPORARY SCENE

Few of today's top-flight conductors stand out as role models for the Armchair Conductor in the manner of the early greats. Is it because the modern jet-age music man is too busy guest conducting, recording, and job hopping, never staying in one place long enough to develop a character worthy of emulation? Or is it because they just don't make 'em like they used to?

Whatever the reason, don't write off the whole current crop. Some of today's conductors are worth looking to. You may find inspiration or a kindred spirit among these:

- **All-American Boy:**
    Leonard Slatkin not only attends St. Louis Cardinal baseball games with a passion he otherwise reserves for Rachmaninoff, but he's been known to throw out the first ball at Busch Stadium wearing a tux and a Cards cap, and he

sometimes announces scores from the podium midconcert.

- **Recording Superstar No. 1:**
Sir Neville Marriner boasts an output of recordings that's so prolific and receives so much airplay that many thousands of classical-music radio listeners, upon hearing the name Neville, reflexively respond: ". . . Marriner, conducting the Academy of St. Martin-in-the-Fields."

- **Recording Superstar No. 2:**
When it comes to Grammys, Sir Georg Solti has it all over everyone from Frank Sinatra and the Beatles to Michael Jackson and Madonna: He's won an amazing twenty-eight.

● Different Drummer:
Carlos Kleiber, although rated by some as the world's greatest living conductor, has done it his way by refusing to tie himself down with a permanent gig or a greedy gaggle of guest shots, insisting: "I only conduct when I am hungry."

● Child Star:
Lorin Maazel started conducting at age eight and led Toscanini's NBC Symphony at eleven. (Fifty years later, he's music director of the Pittsburgh Symphony and a guest conductor in demand around the world. His career is a model for the young Armchair Conductor, who can look forward to half a century wielding a baton.)

WOMEN ON THE PODIUM

A generation ago, it was said by many that the world wasn't ready for women in certain positions of authority—reading the evening news on network television, for instance, or leading an orchestra.

Today, no woman yet holds a top-level conducting post. But things *have* changed from the bad old sexist days—at least in some areas. Catherine Comet's daughter was raised watching her mother on the podium. Not too long ago, when she was five and her mother was assistant director of the St. Louis Symphony, the little girl went for the first time to a regular subscription concert, conducted by Mom's boss, Leonard Slatkin. The girl was startled. "Mommy!" she cried, after the opening applause had died. "It's a man!"

*Maestra
Catherine Comet*

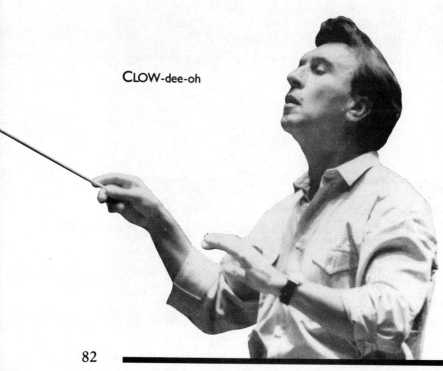

CLOW-dee-oh

SPEAKING OF CONDUCTORS

One of the tricks of carrying yourself well as an Armchair Conductor is having a basic name-dropping vocabulary—knowing the names of prominent practitioners. Just recognizing them in print won't do. You have to know how to pronounce them.

Some of the names here you've probably been saying wrong for years. It's high time you learned. Remember:

James Levine is leh-VINE, not leh-VEEN.

And **Leonard Bernstein** is BURN-stine, not BURN-steen, although he started as BURN-steen. (But then, before he was Leonard, he was Louis—he kept the last, changed the first.)

George Szell is SELL, not ZELL, and he's plain George.

Sir Georg Solti is SHOAL-tee, not SOAL-tee, and he's also George (although purists favor GAY-ork).

Leopold Stokowski is LAY-oh-pold, not LEE-oh-pold, and, of course, sto-KOFF-skee, never sto-COW-skee. "There is no *cow* in my name," the maestro used to complain. (For a time, he even took to spelling it *Stokovski*, but gave that up.)

Leonard Slatkin, preferring American ways, is SLAT-kin, not SLOT-kin.

Claudio Abbado is CLOW-dee-oh, not CLAW-dee-oh.

Bernard Haitink is HY-tink, not HAY-tink.

Ernest Ansermet is said the French way: AIR-nest AW(N)-sair-may.

Charles Dutoit too: SHARL dü-TWAH. (The dü uses the French *u* sound, a puckered *ee*.)

SHARL dü-TWAH

Pierre Monteux is *not* moan-TOE or even moan-TOO; say moa(n)-TE(R)—that's nasal on the first syllable, the second syllable sounding like the end of "deter" without the *r*.
And **Riccardo Chailly** is shy-YEE.
Antal Dorati leans on the DOR: DOR-ah-tee.
But **Lorin Maazel** leans on the ZEL: mah-ZEL.
Eugen Jochum is OY-ghen YO-khum (with a hard *g* and a gutteral *ch*).
Kurt Masur is KOORT mah-ZOOR.
Catherine Comet is koh-MAY, not KAH-met.

But **Pierre Boulez** is boo-LEHZ, not boo-LAY.
Christoph (and it *isn't* Christopher) **von Dohnányi** likes the German *fun* but the Hungarian DOKH-nahn-yee.
Herbert von Karajan is HAIR-burt fun CAR-ah-yahn.

fun DOKH-nahn-yee

84

Edo de Waart is A-doe duh-VAHRT.
Esa-Pekka Salonen is ES-uh PEK-uh SAH-lo-nen.
Wolfgang Sawallisch is VAWLF-gahng (please, no English *w*, no English *a*) suh-VAHL-ish.
Neeme Järvi is NAY-muh YAHR-vee.
And **Mstislav Rostropovich** is (deep breath) mis-to-SLAHV ro-stro-POH-vitch).

And now, the postgraduate course: Better than avoiding pronunciation goofs is knowing how to avoid conductors' names altogether. If you use their nicknames, you not only avoid tangling your tongue but show off your knowledge of inside information.

To those in the know, for instance, the multisyllabic Mr. Rostropovich is simply

A-doe duh-VAHRT

"Slava." Pierre Boulez has been called "Charlie the Tuna" (after his mania for having instruments tuned). Stokowski was always "Stoki." Not just British musicians but fans knew Sir Malcolm Sargent as "Flash Harry."

In opera circles, "Jimmy" means only Levine. "Lenny"—need it be said?—still means Bernstein and Bernstein only. (Leonard Slatkin knows this, which is why he says *he* is "Leonard, because there's only one 'Lenny.'") Michael Tilson Thomas is "M.T.T." Zubin Mehta has heard "Zubie Baby" more than once, but probably not to his face.

"Maestro" is always appropriate.

M.T.T.

Zubie Baby

ON THE BANDSTAND

In the world of big dance and pop bands, an era that's almost—but not quite—gone, a steady rhythm section frequently took care of much of the conductor's job, but someone had to front the band anyway.

Bob Crosby, Bing's little brother, who named his band after himself: the Bobcats ◄

Paul Whiteman, the "King of Jazz," who introduced George Gershwin's Rhapsody in Blue in 1924 ►

Whoops!

As an Armchair Conductor, you have the luxury of being able to mess up totally without causing too much fuss or embarrassment. If you really blow it, console yourself with the thought that disaster has struck all the greats of the baton. Some examples to make you feel a little more comfortable—and to make you smile:

- Like many composers, Antonin Dvořák sometimes conducted his own works. He led his *Stabat Mater* many times—perhaps once too often. One memorable evening, halfway through the piece, he fell asleep on the podium.
- Daniel Türk, an early-nineteenth-century organist who also did some conducting, once suffered a much noisier mishap. So energetic was his baton work that he overdid an upbeat, smashed his stick into the chandelier over his head, and showered the orchestra with broken glass.
- Charles Dutoit also let a baton slip out of his hand during a performance, but it didn't break a chandelier. It flew into the audience and got stuck in a spectator's hairdo.
- While it may be acceptable to be an absentminded composer, it can be embarrassing to be an absentminded conductor. Johannes Brahms learned that sad fact the night he forgot to button his suspenders before mounting the podium. His pants fell down.
- Sir Landon Ronald was also done in by a memory lapse. He changed a symphony program, subbing Wagner's *Tannhäuser* for Mendelssohn's *A Midsummer Night's Dream*. When he reached the podium, he forgot about the

switch. Sir Landon gave the downbeat for the Mendelssohn. The orchestra started the Wagner. Sir Landon fainted.

● Boris Sirpo recovered nicely from a small mishap that might have embarrassed a conductor with slower reflexes. On a key gesture at a crucial moment in Strauss's "Death and Transfiguration," he accidentally hit his music stand with the baton. A few inches of the end snapped off and flew straight up. Never slowing his baton, Sirpo stuck out his left hand and snagged the fragment on its way down—right on the beat.

Nobody's Perfect

He was a composer, primarily, and like many composers he liked to conduct his own works, especially premieres. But while as a composer he was pretty good, as a conductor he was...well...

- His style was, to say the least, excitable. For soft passages, he would bend down, "almost under the desk," according to one observer. For loud parts, he stood on tiptoe or leapt into the air, sometimes shouting to the orchestra for good measure.
- His memory was spotty. One time he forgot that he had ordered the orchestra *not* to repeat a certain section of music. At the performance he went back, they went on, and the whole piece ground to a halt as he hollered, "Stop! Wrong! That will not do! Again! Again!"
- Tales were told, but disputed by some, about a time he was conducting and performing his own piano concerto: forgetting that he was playing, he jumped up from the bench, started waving his arms about, and knocked the candles off the piano. Another time, he knocked down a choirboy.
- His hearing was never very good, but as it worsened, musicians began to dread his conducting. They tried ignoring him and taking cues from the head violinist, but he managed to interfere and wreck the performances anyway. One time, during a long soft passage, which he couldn't hear, he lost count; when he jumped high for a loud passage, nothing happened because he was much too early for the volume change.
- Finally, his hearing became so far gone that all delicacy was thrust aside in favor of the music. He was asked to please go home and not conduct ever again. Which is what he did.

He was Ludwig van Beethoven.

OUT OF THE ARMCHAIR

Can an Armchair Conductor leap from the realm of fantasy to a real wooden podium with real, live musicians ready to do their leader's bidding? Ah, to make the strings sing, to shake hands firmly with the concertmaster, to take a deep bow in front of a wildly cheering audience, to return for yet another bow and—can it even be breathed? —perhaps an encore!

Nice dream.

In the 1940s and 1950s, bandleader Sammy Kaye invited audience members to take his baton in a show segment called "So You Want to Lead a Band." The band followed the wannabes' gestures to a T, resulting, of course, in a major mess almost every time.

Today, some bands and orchestras occasionally invite outsiders to try their hand at conducting—usually as a fund-raiser. The Boston Pops, for instance, has a standing offer to contributors: Give us $5,000 and you get to lead the orchestra's signature piece, "The Stars and Stripes Forever," at a regular concert—rehearsal time included.

The greatest success story for a dreamer is that of Gilbert Kaplan, founder and chairman of *Institutional Investor* magazine. Although hardly a musician—he took piano lessons for just three years as a boy—Kaplan began a love affair with Mahler's immensely difficult *Resurrection* Symphony and let it gnaw at him until he decided, at age forty, to do something about it. Although he was advised that "you can't possibly conduct Mahler until you've conducted Haydn," Kaplan put his money where his armchair was: he hired a live-in conductor and went to work. They spent up to nine hours a day drilling on everything from the basics of baton waving to the fine points of the ninety-minute work. They made trips to Amsterdam and Tokyo to scrutinize performances of the piece. He hired the American Symphony Orchestra for a dozen full rehearsals.

Gilbert Kaplan, out of his armchair

At last, he rented Avery Fisher Hall in New York, signed 119 instrumentalists and 200 singers, and scheduled his debut to coincide with his magazine's fifteenth anniversary. (Tax deductible.) Because he couldn't read a score, he conducted from memory.

Not only did the fairy-tale concert come off well (one critic sneaked into the closed black-tie concert performance; he liked it), but it launched Kaplan on a conducting career with a repertory of one: he's led the symphony more than a dozen and a half times in concert halls around the world. His 1988 recording, with the London Symphony Orchestra, has reportedly sold more than a hundred thousand copies, a best seller in the world of classics, an especially monstrous hit for a Mahler work.

Other Armchair Conductors who have gotten out of their armchairs include Big Bird and the Famous San Diego Chicken. The

Bird, at eight feet two the world's tallest conductor, has led many orchestras in the United States, Canada, and Australia, although his musical training consists of "just a little twittering in the trees."

The Chicken once led the Denver Symphony Orchestra. When his debut was announced, detractors wondered aloud if he could pullet off. With his poultry talent, some groused, the only stick he can handle is a drumstick. Others went so far as to predict that he'd fowl up and lay an egg on the podium. But did the Chicken get in a stew? No. Never one to duck a challenge—especially when his opponents are turkeys—he chose to put on his tails and wing it. The Chicken was a hit. Critics praised his good taste and his extra crispy baton technique. In the end, everyone agreed the performance was a feather in his cap.

The San Diego Chicken with the Denver Symphony Orchestra

ARTHUR NIKISCH

TELLS ALL HE KNOWS ABOUT CONDUCTING WHILE STANDING ON ONE FOOT

Arthur Nikisch

Arthur Nikisch was a giant of the conducting world a century ago. One day as he was entering the concert hall in Leipzig, he was waylaid by a young man who begged the legendary maestro to take him on as a student. "Of course, I'd be glad to," Nikisch replied. "It's really very easy." The conductor waved his right arm in the familiar baton patterns. "One-two-three-four, one-two-three, one-two," he said solemnly. "The rest you have to do yourself."

A TIP OF THE BATON TO . . .

Brown Miggs and Tom Evered, Angel/EMI; Allen Arrow; Tim Baker; Peter Berinstein; Marilyn Egol, BMG Classics; Suzie Bonton and Ken Haas, BSO; Elaine Durnin Boughner; Joseph Bulova School of Watchmaking; The Carson Office; Center for Safety in the Arts; Brenda Nelson-Strauss, Chicago Symphony Orchestra; Richard Lederman, The Cleveland Clinic; Carol Jacobs, The Cleveland Orchestra; Clare Avery, Colbert Artists Management; Michael Comin; Howard Denike; Rafaela Hernández and Jennifer Heinlein, DGG; Jane Bernard for The Famous Chicken; Michael Feingold; Hunter Fry; Sheila Hall; Jay K. Hoffman Associates (for Virgin Classics); Stan Kremen; Ben Lunzer; Paul Gunther, Minnesota Orchestra; Movie Star News; Mary Corliss, MOMA; Chris Willard and Barbara Haws, New York Philharmonic Archives; New York Public Library; Jack Topchik, *The New York Times*; Susan Marmie, Oregon Symphony; Cathie Osborne; Gus Parras Archives; The Philadelphia Orchestra; Sylvia Turner, Pittsburgh Symphony; PolyGram Records; Ted Prochazka; Scott Dine, *St. Louis Post-Dispatch*; Joan Briccetti, St. Louis Symphony; Hugh Kaylor, Shaw Concerts; Philip DuBois, Sony Classical; Peter Thompson; Walter Wager; Sonja Weiss, Mario Mazza, WNCN-FM; and especially Nancy Carlinsky and Helene Goodgold.

Technical advisor: Elias Dann, Ph.D., professor of music, Florida State University. For any lapses, do not blame him; forgive the authors.

Photo and drawing credits: CBS Records, The Philadelphia Orchestra, Archives of the Musical Arts Association, Steven J. Sherman (2), Clive Barda/Columbia Records, Boston Symphony Orchestra (2), J. Hayter, Boulanger, Ape/*Vanity Fair*, Schliessmann (3), David Farrell, Peter Keller/ Phonogram International, Chicago Symphony Orchestra (2), Alex von Koettlitz, Jörg Reichardt, Evan Wilcox, Wiedemann, Enrico Caruso, Edmund Dulac, Heinz Karnine/Angel Records, S. Lauterwasser, Mike Evans/ Phonogram International, Vivianne Rome, Schaffler, Robert Mastroianni, Christina Burton, *The New York Times*, Robert Sterl, Roullet after Mignard.

Original line art: Nick Lynn, Moffitt Cecil, Scott Bodie.

Music snippets: Doloris C. Milone.

Interior Design: Michaelis/Carpelis Design Assoc. Inc.

Warning!

Conducting may be hazardous to your health. More than a few celebrated conductors—including Sir Thomas Beecham, Otto Klemperer, Pierre Monteux, and Leonard Bernstein—have fallen off the podium while conducting. Leonard Slatkin and Sir Georg Solti, among others, have drawn

The unfortunate Jean Baptiste Lully

blood during heated performances by stabbing themselves with their own batons.

But the conductor who really took it on the chin was Giovanni Battista Lulli, an Italian orphan who learned to fiddle, moved to France, changed his name to Jean Baptiste Lully, and ended up as court music maven to Louis XIV. As famous in his day for his temper as for his talent, the super-strict Lully kept time for the king's orchestra by pounding on the floor in rhythm with a stick as tall as he was and with a crown on top. In 1687, leading a Te Deum performed in gratitude for the recovery of His Majesty from a severe illness, Lully—whether from ecstasy or rage is not known—clobbered his foot with the staff. The foot swelled and developed gangrene. Lully took to his bed, where he composed a hymn, "Sinner, Thou Must Die," which he sang to friends in a weak, shaky voice. A few days later, he became the first recorded case of death by conducting.